Two Fat Men

A light-hearted drama

Gillian Plowman

Samuel French—London
New York-Toronto-Hollywood

Please see page iv for further copyright information

TWO FAT MEN

First performed by Flat Four with the following cast:

Duncan	Robert Iles
Julie	Gillian Plowman
Molly	Jenny Armstrong
Marion	Lorna Allen
Fiona	Frances Iles
George	David Flint
Phœbe	Iris Bartle
Jerome	Daryl Bennett

Directed by Karrie Stark

CHARACTERS

Duncan, an overweight fisherman with a jokey nature
Julie, a successful Weight Buster, a determined leader
Molly, Julie's "second-in-command", a reliable Weight Buster
Marion, trying hard; a vulnerable Weight Buster
Fiona, an attractive, "getting-there" Weight Buster
George, an overweight IBM man who doesn't want to be there
Phoebe, a deaf and dumb sign teacher
Jerome, Julie's son, a "scrawny sod"

The action of the play takes place in the room outside the
Weight Busters' meeting place

Time — the present

SIGN LANGUAGE

For help with the sign language used in this play, producers are
advised to contact either:

RNID (Royal National Institute for the Deaf)
19-23 Featherstone Street
London EC1Y 8SL

or

SPIT (Signed Performances in Theatre)
1 Stobart Avenue
Prestwich
Manchester
M25 0AJ

*Other plays by Gillian Plowman
published by Samuel French Ltd:*

Beata Beatrix
Cecily
Close to Croydon
David's Birthday
The Janna Years
A Kind of Vesuvius
Me and My Friend
Philip and Rowena
There's None So Blind
Tippers
Two Summers
Unjama Land

TWO FAT MEN

The room outside the Weight Busters' meeting place

It is the reception room/foyer of an old town house, still rather grand but now rather practical, being used as a meeting place for community projects. There are two small tables with information leaflets on them; chairs are grouped around each table. The entrance from outside — and to other rooms — is L; *the entrance to the meeting place is* R

Duncan enters L, *not sure where to go*

Julie enters R *and sweeps through, looking at her watch*

Julie Are you with me? Julie, your leader? Weight Busters?
Duncan Yes. No.
Julie (*smiling encouragingly*)Yes, you are. Duncan … ?
Duncan Yes.
Julie Don't worry. Look, I'll just go and get organized and come back for you. You've made the first step and that's the big one. The first step. You've made a great decision. There's another man starting tonight. Another great decision maker. Why don't you wait for him? Chum up and come in together? Group support is a vital part of what Weight Busters is all about. Telling others how you feel and sharing problems and solutions will really help to keep you motivated.
Duncan Will it?
Julie Believe it. And believe this. *I* really care. About you and your weight loss. And I will be here every week. For you. Julie. (*She holds out her hand*)

Duncan and Julie shake hands

(*Smiling at Duncan with great encouragement*) Now, do this for me. When the other new man arrives, make him feel part of you. Part of a new adventure you're both setting out on. This is going to change both your lives, I can feel it – in more ways than either of us know. So you sit here and wait a few minutes, but don't get too comfortable! Exciting times ahead … Remember, I care.

Julie goes on her way and exits L

Duncan sits

Molly and Marion, two (large) ladies, enter R and head across the room, following Julie

Molly (*to Duncan; breezily*) Hallo!
Duncan (*breezily back*) Hallo!
Marion Hallo!
Duncan Hallo!

Fiona, a third large lady, enters R and runs after Molly and Marion

Fiona (*calling*) Julie! We're in the blue room tonight. They've put sign language in our usual.

Julie enters L

Julie Sign language. That's new.
Fiona Yes. A new class. I was thinking of doing it.
Julie Not on a Weight Busters night!

Fiona scuttles back R past Duncan

Fiona Hallo!
Duncan Hallo!
Molly Hallo again! (*She taps Duncan on the knee*)
Marion Hallo!

Duncan Hallo!
Marion We're a very friendly bunch.

Julie, Molly, Marion and Fiona bundle into the room R

George enters

Duncan (*before he can stop himself; breezily*) Hallo!

George looks sick

Sorry. (*More subdued*) Hallo.

George nods. He is uncertain where to go

(*Discreetly*) Are you here for … ?
George (*sharply*) What?
Duncan What I'm here for?
George What are you here for?

Duncan pats his tummy

(*Looking round*) What else is there?
Duncan Sign language.
George I can do sign language.
Duncan Can you?
George What do you want? One finger or two?
Duncan Ah.
George What? Ah what?

Beat

Duncan We're to wait here.
George (*sitting down*) Why?
Duncan Go in together.
George Go in where together?
Duncan Come on, come clean. (*He whispers*) Weight Busters.

George How did you know I was coming?
Duncan Julie told me. Our leader.
George I nearly didn't. In fact, I'm going. (*He gets up*)
Duncan So am I then.
George What?
Duncan If you're going, I'm going. (*He gets up*)
George Right then. (*He sits*) I can't go. My wife dropped me off so I couldn't escape in the car. She's picking me up. (*He looks at his watch and groans*)

Duncan sits. George and Duncan look at each other, feeling silly. They look as if they recognize each other — possibly

George I know you, don't I?
Duncan I think so, yes …

They shake hands

Yes.

George wants to put a name to Duncan but can't. Duncan wants to put a name to George but can't

George Never forget a face.
Duncan Names. (*He shakes his head*)
George Names. (*He shakes his head*)

George wants to put a name to Duncan but can't. Duncan wants to put a name to George but can't

George George Kingworthy. (*He holds his hand out again*)

They shake hands

Duncan Duncan Bridges.

This means nothing to George

George Doesn't ring a bell.

Duncan No bells.

George You don't work at IBM, do you?

Duncan No. Do you?

George (*nodding*) Big place. You see lots of people. Never know their names.

Duncan Computers?

George The best.

Duncan Got one at home.

George Have you?

Duncan Very satisfied with it. Games! Music! CD ROMs! Internet! *Stuff* you can get on the internet! E-mails. I'm communicating with my kids now. They're very high-tech in London, Manchester and Wiveliscombe.

George Where's that?

Duncan Somerset. My wife gets upset though.

George She can't spell it.

Duncan What?

George My wife can't spell either.

Duncan I think my wife's all right with Wiveliscombe.

George Why is she upset then?

Duncan I get in from work and log on.

George Empty nest syndrome. They've all gone, so you've got to pay attention to her.

Duncan That's it!

George Count yourself lucky. My wife couldn't have any kids so I've spent me life paying attention to her.

Duncan That's a shame.

George What?

Duncan Not having kids. For you.

George Probably got one or two knocking around somewhere!

Duncan Really?

George I don't know, do I? What I get fed up about is ... I love my wife — but I wish she'd do something really interesting so that I can admire her. I'd like to admire her.

Duncan I admire her. For living with you.

George Bastard ...

Duncan My wife wants me to go — line dancing.
George I've been ... No, I haven't.
Duncan What?
George Nothing.
Duncan Line dancing?
George No.
Duncan I'm only doing *this* to get out of *that*.

George "humphs"

Do you fancy going to the pub?
George What now?
Duncan Yes.
George Get thee behind me, Satan.

Duncan moves behind George

Duncan Do you fancy going to the pub? We can be back in time
to be picked up.
George I tell you what. If we can't bear it, we'll go to the pub.
Duncan After how long?
George Half an hour.
Duncan It won't take that long.

Phœbe enters L *and talks to them in sign language*

Phœbe (*signing*) Can you tell me where they're holding the sign
language class.
Duncan The sign language room is that way. (*He points* L *and
smiles*)

Phœbe is pleased. She thanks Duncan and goes off L

George How did you know what she said?
Duncan Obvious, wasn't it?

George thinks about that. He looks at his watch

George Are we supposed to go in?
Duncan What, be self-motivated?

There is a long pause. They don't move

George What do you do? Work?
Duncan Well, that's the point. I'm out all day. Out. Outdoors out. Fishing.
George No!
Duncan (*surprised*) Yes.
George Fishing?
Duncan Yes.
George That's wonderful.
Duncan Bit cold and bloody wet sometimes. Which is why I like to sit in front of my warm and cosy computer ...
George I fish.
Duncan For IBM?
George For the antidote. The antithesis. The antitoxin to IBM. For warm and cosy read stifling, suffocating. Man the hunter must re-emerge and face the elements. Weekends when I don't have to go into the office — I fish off the beach, and by night, the stillness of the canal bank is intoxicating. Upsets my wife.
Duncan Not enough attention.

A moment of understanding

Why don't you take her with you.
George Fishing?
Duncan Supposed to do things together.
George So why don't you go line dancing?
Duncan (*suspiciously*) You've *been* line dancing!
George No, I haven't!
Duncan Seems like it to me.
George Is that where we met?
Duncan I haven't been yet.
George I haven't. I *haven't*. Watched others.

Silence

Did your wife want to come with you?

Duncan Where?

George Here.

Duncan No. Apparently, Julie said, "Don't come with him. He has to do this for himself. I will make him over," Julie said.

George So your wife organized it?

Duncan Didn't yours?

George I love my wife.

Duncan Didn't answer the question.

George Yes it did.   ·

Pause

Duncan So — where've we met then?

Pause

George You been in prison?

Duncan I have, yes. Taken fish in.

George Slippery customers.

Duncan Have you?

George I don't catch that many. (*Beat*) No. Not counting IBM.

Duncan Hospital? I've had my appendix out.

George Taken grapes in.

Duncan Maybe you visited me when I had my appendix out?

They know they're talking rubbish

George So where's this Julie?

Duncan Preparing for us. (*Beat*) They weigh us, you know.

George Shit.

Duncan Shit.

They look at each other, assessing each other's weight, then each of them looks at his own body. They both hope the other is heavier

Molly enters R

Molly Hallo again! I'm Molly. Sort of second-in-command. 'Cos I've been coming the longest. Julie says to see if you're both here, and if you are, to go back and tell her. (*To George*) Now you're Duncan?
George No.
Duncan (*helpfully*) George.
Molly (*to Duncan*) You're George?
Duncan No, Duncan.
Molly We all care, you know.

Molly exits

George Nice bottom.
Duncan Thank you.

They titter

We don't live in the same street, do we?
George Cathedral Close.
Duncan Don't live in the same town.
George Where do you live then?
Duncan Bognor. Wasn't going to their one — you know. Might be recognized.
George I recognized you here.
Duncan We don't know that yet.

George studies Duncan

George Yes!
Duncan What?
George I know where it was! We went — do you remember — there was that snookerthon something a couple of years ago — all-night thing, we were playing all night and — at the umm — pub — in Bognor — you know — and we got chatting at the bar — putting the world to rights — charity thing — remember? That was it.

Duncan is completely blank

George and Dragon. That was it. You beat me, you bastard.

Duncan I don't remember that.

George You beat me.

Duncan Never been in the *George and Dragon.* Which *George and Dragon*?

George It *was* you. The *George and Dragon.* You know. On the front. At Bognor.

Duncan Never been in there. Yes I have.

George There you are!

Duncan For my wedding reception. Never been back.

George When was that then?

Duncan What?

George Your wedding reception?

Duncan Just after my wedding. (*He doesn't remember how long ago it was*) You didn't come to my wedding?

George I would only have come to your wedding if I *knew* you, wouldn't I?

Duncan Or my wife.

George What's your wife's name?

Duncan Or my in-laws. They did all the inviting. Fiona.

George Fiona what?

Duncan Bridges.

George I knew a Fiona *Mills.* Tarty little thing. Very generous with it. When I say I *knew* her, I *knew* her … You know, I didn't appreciate what I had in my hands. Looking back, Fiona Mills is just what I need now. Course Fiona Mills wouldn't be now what Fiona Mills was then — seventeen years old and pointed. Very pointy bras they had, remember them? Fiona Mills lived in Bognor …

Duncan's face falls

Oh bloody hell. Oh Douglas.

Duncan Duncan.

George Duncan. You didn't marry Fiona Mills, did you?

Duncan crumples

I didn't mean it. She was just, I mean she wasn't *just* … I really liked her, you know … Just talk. Oh shit. Sorry.

Duncan Fiona Lovatt.

George Lovatt.

Duncan Lovatt. My wife's maiden name. (*He grins wickedly at George*)

George You bastard.

Duncan That's three times you've called me a bastard.

George Well, you are, letting me think ——

Duncan You go on about loving your wife and all the time you're fancying someone else.

George I fancy *being* someone else. Someone different. Which is why I'm here. My wife says I *could* be someone different. Someone three stones lighter. She doesn't like being squashed, you see. She's Scottish.

Beat

Duncan Mac something?

George Hannah Mac something. She was. Kingworthy now. Much better.

Duncan Can you understand her?

George Rarely.

Duncan I never can.

George Do you know her?

Duncan The Scots. Beyond me.

George You're xenophobic.

Duncan It's only the Scots. I like the Japanese.

George Why?

Duncan They eat raw fish.

George They think they've conquered the computer world.

Duncan No, IBM think they've conquered the computer world.

George I hope we weren't at school together.

Duncan Why?

George There's a sort of outlook that your school gives you.

Duncan The gasworks.

George That's what I mean. The outlook that can only see the gasworks.

Duncan You mean you're a snob.

George I just had a good education. Private. I'm not ashamed of it, although these days, you're supposed to be. You get to know more than just the basics …

Duncan I'm not asking. I don't want to know. I don't like the sound of you.

George You haven't heard it.

Duncan What?

George The sound of me.

Duncan What sound?

George sings a verse of Gilbert and Sullivan's He Is An Englishman

George That's the sort of education I had.

Duncan sings the next verse of He Is An Englishman

Duncan I wish I'd had an education like you.

George and Duncan stand and sing together to the end of the song, rousingly

Jerome enters during their rendition and hears them

George Do you sing?

Duncan On the boat. What about you?

George On the beach.

Jerome Are there singing classes here?

George No.

Duncan Sign language?

Jerome Is Weight Busters in the usual place?

Jerome turns to exit into the room L

George It works, then.

Duncan (*calling after Jerome*) It's that way. (*He points* R)

George How long does it take to look like that, do you think?

Jerome turns and moves R

Julie enters from the room R

Jerome and Julie bump into each other

Julie (*to Duncan and George*) Now you have my full ——
Jerome Mum.
Julie (*to Jerome*) What?
Jerome Could you let me have some money please?
Julie (*to Duncan and George*) — attention.
Jerome Please, Mum.
Julie Jerome, I'm at work. (*To Duncan and George*) I know what it has taken for you to come here.
Jerome Do you know what it has taken for *me* to come here?
Julie (*to Jerome*) Yes, a bloody cheek. You don't pay me any lodging, you don't pay for any food ——
Jerome I'm not earning.
Julie Exactly. You don't go out and get a job.
Jerome I've got an audition on Friday. I just need to go to this last singing lesson. Then I'll be earning.
Julie You expect to earn a living singing?
Jerome And dancing. You can't just be an actor, these days, you have to be an all-rounder.
Julie All-round failure, Jerome. You haven't got a part yet.
Jerome It takes time.
Julie Eternity.
Jerome Why don't you have any faith in me?
Julie (*to Duncan and George*) You tell me, what has it taken for you to come here? Duncan? And … ?
Duncan George.
Jerome I'll get this one, I know it.
Julie (*to Jerome*) No! Why don't you pay for your own singing lessons? Work in a pub. Or McDonald's. Somewhere …
Jerome I need to focus.
Julie (*to Duncan and George*) A will, a need, a want, a determination to lose weight. Am I right?

Jerome A focus.

Julie Yes, a focus. Shut up, Jerome.

George A wife.

Duncan Yes, it's — er — more a wife really.

Jerome Don't let your lives be ruled by women. Don't get involved with my mother.

Julie Wives who care about you. About your health and your looks. Who did they marry, eh? Slim, handsome, *virile* young blades? They want them back. Think about it. All the things you'll be able to do without losing your breath, things that your wives will appreciate, mmm? It's not difficult. I'll guide you through. I'll look after you. I care.

Jerome She emasculated my father. She rules by fear and blackmail and vicious tongue.

Julie Bugger off, Jerome, you scrawny sod. I'm not giving you any more money. You take after your father … (*To George and Duncan*) I'm sorry about this. His father — took every penny I had …

Jerome He *borrowed* it.

Julie He never paid me back.

Jerome Because *he* borrowed it.

Julie "It's a medical thing," he said … "it'll put me right and I'll be able to work again. I'll pay you back" your father said.

Jerome But *she* didn't see why she should.

Julie *She* was the reason he stopped working.

Jerome He couldn't help being made redundant.

Julie He got the sack!

Jerome And you went on and on at him. Have you been to the Job Centre? Who have you written to? What's in the job page? You haven't cooked the supper, you could have done the ironing … He hid from you!

Julie Why don't you hide from me!

Jerome He was terrified of you!

Julie Well, that just shows you how much of a man he was.

Jerome (*to Duncan and George*) You're terrified of your wives, aren't you?

George No.

Duncan No.
Jerome Then what the hell are you doing here?

George and Duncan look at each other

   Wasting an evening of your lives here when you could be ——
George Fishing.
Duncan Surfing the internet.
Jerome Singing!
George Yes, singing …
Julie How dare you. You parasite, you. They are my living. They are mine.
Jerome See, see? She thinks she owns you already. Your lives won't be your own.
Julie They're here of their own free will.
Jerome Doesn't seem that way to me.
Julie They know I can improve the quality of their lives.
Jerome That's what women think, you see. Think they know best. There's nothing wrong in being fat.
Julie That's easy to say when you're thin.
Jerome Look at Pavarotti.
Julie He's on a diet!
Jerome You too can be thin if you let your lives be nagged away. Like my father.
Julie Go and ride your bloody hobby horse somewhere else.
Jerome You won't emasculate me.
Julie That's a favourite word, isn't?
Jerome That's what you did to him.
Julie It was the other way round.
Jerome When he stopped bringing money home, through no fault of his own, you persecuted him.
Julie (*to Duncan and George*) His father took all my savings and had a sex change operation!

Duncan and George look uncomfortable

Jerome If you can't beat 'em, join 'em!

Julie He turned into a beautiful woman and I turned into the fattest, ugliest creature on earth.

Jerome Got the photo?

Julie gets out a photograph of herself as a fat woman and shows it to George and Duncan

Julie That's what I looked like. That's what I was. That's what he did to me! His womanhood made a mockery of mine. I went up to eighteen stone because of the shock and the shame. So I know what it's like. I've been there. That's why I can help you.

Duncan I haven't got to eighteen stone, have you?

George No.

Julie You will. If you don't take this opportunity to save yourselves.

Jerome She's getting evangelical now.

Julie We're all addicted, we all adore something and everything on this earth can be worshipped. You fall in love with what you focus on. People fall in love with food.

Molly, Marion and Fiona emerge

Molly Julie, are you all right?

Jerome She's going through another sainthood.

Julie (*shouting*) Fall in love with something else! Go on, all of you. Go and do something else! I don't care if you get fatter and fatter. That's up to you. Why should I care, week after week, listening to your tales of woe, your pathetic excuses … Piss off, all of you, and get a life.

Julie turns and exits

There is silence

George (*to Jerome*) You're a little git, aren't you?

Jerome She doesn't usually … She usually just gives me twenty-five quid.

Fiona Perhaps she hasn't got it. Have you thought of that?

Molly Go after her, Jerome. See if she's all right.
Jerome Yes. Sorry … I think you should sing, though. I think it's important. Sorry.

Jerome exits

Marion It's my fault.
Molly No, it's not, Marion.
Marion I never told Julie before, and I came tonight saying to myself, I know she really cares and it would be … Well it would be helpful — for her to know why I am like I am — because she could help me better — if I told her … I got convicted of shop-lifting last year. I had to go to court and stand there whilst they said what I stole. My husband was really angry and his mother said, "See – I told you she wasn't good enough for you." And she had him home again. And he took Bruno.
Molly Who's Bruno?
Marion My dog. I didn't care any more after that. That's why I got fat. Comfort eating. And not having a dog to take for walks. So I told her. She's right. It's pathetic.
Fiona Oh, Marion.

Fiona gives Marion a hug

What did you — umm — lift?
Molly Externalize it, Marion.
Marion A tennis racket.
Molly Do you play tennis?
Marion No. I wasn't allowed to keep it. And some underwear.
Molly We understand.
Marion And some bacon.

Duncan and George clearly hate all this

And a bunch of tulips. Nobody ever gives me flowers.
Duncan Or bacon.
Marion No.

Fiona It's not just you, Marion.

Marion I shouldn't have pounced on her first thing.

Fiona It's me she meant. Pathetic.

Marion Why?

Fiona I phoned her up today ... I mean, why should I phone Julie? Why burden her with it?

Marion What?

Fiona This is going to sound really silly. I've been writing to this man. And he thinks I'm five foot seven, blonde and slim — and sexy — and I never thought I'd have to meet him, but now he's got parole and he'll find out I'm not.

Marion What?

Fiona Tall and blonde and slim and sexy. So I phoned Julie ——

Molly You can wear high heels, and dye your hair. And you've nearly reached your goal weight ——

Fiona I'm not sexy though.

Molly Yes, you are (*To Duncan*) What do you think, Dudley?

Duncan Duncan.

Fiona I know I'm not sexy.

Duncan George?

George What?

Duncan Answer the question.

George The thing is ... The thing is — I do *know* what sexy is — because ... well, the sexiest — person — I ever met was ... (*To Duncan*) Are we going to the pub?

Duncan Is it half an hour?

George Seems like half a lifetime.

Molly *Was ... ?*

George And yes, I would say you are. Yes.

Molly Was *who*?

George Fiona Mills.

Fiona stands stock still and stares at George. The following line is greeted with a deathly hush

Duncan And that was because she had very pointy —— (*He stops himself as he realizes the hush has fallen*)

George What?
Duncan What?
Fiona That's me.
George What?
Fiona I was Fiona Mills.

Duncan and George cannot stop themselves looking at Fiona's breasts and away again

Before I was married. And now I'm divorced, I'm Fiona Mills again. So, who are you?
George Umm ...
Duncan George Kingworthy.
Fiona *You* are?
Duncan *He* is.
Fiona George Kingworthy?
Duncan Was, is and ever shall be.

Fiona slaps George's face

Fiona Bastard! I was only seventeen. Only seventeen! (*She turns to the others as though that explains everything*) He got me pregnant.

Everyone looks at George

George (*totally dismayed*) I didn't know.
Fiona No, because you went off and I never saw you again.
George To university. My parents moved to Guildford at the same time, so I never came back — till fairly recently.
Duncan With IBM.
George Yes. IBM.
Fiona Not IBM? No.
George Well — yes. Sorry. What's wrong with IBM?
Fiona That's his initials. Ian Barry Mills. Your son.
George My son?

There is a deathly hush

I didn't know. I'm really sorry, Fiona. My son. How old is he?

Fiona He would have been twenty-six. He was run over by a car when he was five.

George He died?

Fiona Yes.

George (*overcome, suddenly bereaved*) I never knew … him …

Duncan reluctantly puts an arm round George's shoulders. There is a silence. Marion puts her arm round Fiona's shoulders

Fiona It was a long time ago.

George I loved my son.

Duncan George, you didn't know him.

George I've always loved him. Inside me, I've always known.

Fiona Have you?

George I knew there was somebody. Yes. My son …

Fiona He'd just started school …

There is another silence

George Did you have any other children?

Fiona Two girls. Then my husband left me. You left me. He left me. And Ian Barry left me. I thought there was something wrong with me. That's why I got fat. For years I was fat. Julie got me back again.

There is another silence

Marion When you rang her today, what did she tell you to do about the man on patrol?

Fiona *Parole*. Tell him the truth, she said. She said … (*She can't continue*)

Molly You are a special person. Appreciate yourself for what you are. Like yourself, Fiona.

Fiona I can't.

George Fiona Mills, you have always been the sexiest person I've ever met.

Fiona Is that true?

George And I know that you were the best mother Ian Barry could have had. That you loved him more than any other little boy was ever loved.

Fiona I did. (*She blows her nose*)

Marion blows her nose. As does Molly. As does Duncan

Fiona Do you still dance? You were brilliant at the twist.

Duncan He's brilliant at line dancing now.

George I don't go line dancing.

Molly You will now.

George What?

Molly We stand in a line to be weighed, and because we're in a line … We all dread being weighed so it helps with the stress. Also, if you spend half an hour doing it, you earn three extra points, which means – a KitKat! I'll go and turn the weighing-in music up!

Molly exits into the room R

Soon we hear music coming from the room

Duncan George?

George What?

Duncan You all right?

George Yeah.

Duncan Pub?

George Yeah.

Duncan and George get up to go. Marion and Fiona bar their way

Molly enters

Marion They're trying to leave.

Molly No-one leaves Weight Busters till they're thin!

The girls push the men into a line and they all start line dancing

Follow them, you.

They all dance. It takes a while for the men to get in step

   Do what I do.

The dance progresses successfully. Duncan moves to the front as part of the dance

   Phœbe enters L

Duncan and Phœbe face each other

Phœbe (*signing*) Nobody has come to my class. Do you know why?
Duncan Does anybody know sign language?

There is a general chorus of "No". The dance continues during the following

Duncan stops dancing. He talks to Phœbe, moving his hands in improvized signs

Duncan Can you hear me?
Phœbe (*signing*) No.
Duncan Don't you know anyone here?
Phœbe (*signing*) No. Is it a dancing class?
Duncan We're here because … (*He taps his overweight stomach*)
Phœbe (*signing*) It's very nice. I like heavy people. I can feel them through the floor.
Duncan Don't worry about the floorboards.
Phœbe (*signing*) I can feel the rhythm of heavy people.
Duncan You can't hear the music?
Phœbe (*signing*) No, but I can feel it.
Duncan Do you want to join in then?
Phœbe (*signing*) I can't do it.
Duncan Just copy what everyone else is doing.
Phœbe (*signing*) But where are all the people from the signing class? I'm worried.
Duncan Do you want to write it down?

Phœbe (*signing*) I'll have to check the date. I must have come on
the wrong date or the wrong day.
Duncan Write it down.

*Phœbe takes a notepad and pencil from her pocket. She writes on
the notepad and shows it to Duncan*

Duncan. What's yours?
Phœbe (*signing*) Phœbe. (*She writes it down*)

Duncan reads the note

Duncan How do you do, Phœbe?

They shake hands. Phœbe writes more; Duncan reads it

Duncan I'm a natural? You think I could be an interpreter?

Phœbe nods and writes more; Duncan reads it

Would I come to your sign classes when you find out the right
day? I'll consider it if you come and join the line dancing.
Molly You're very good at communicating.
Duncan That's e-mail, that is. Opens you up.

*Phœbe nods vigorously. She and Duncan join the line dancing, the
others welcoming them. The music swells and they all have a good
time. At the end of the dance George takes Fiona aside*

George I'm really sorry.
Fiona So am I.
George I never had children, you know. He was my only ever one.
I wish I'd known him.
Fiona Wait.

Fiona leaves him and exits into the room R

Phœbe writes another note for Duncan. He takes it

Duncan (*reading*) "I like heavy people dancing. I can feel the
  rhythm through the floor."
Phœbe (*signing*) I like.

Duncan, Marion and Molly copy the signs during the following

Duncan I like.
Phœbe (*signing*) Heavy people dancing.

The others follow

Duncan Heavy people dancing.
Phœbe (*signing*) I can feel the rhythm.

The others follow

Duncan I can feel the rhythm.
Phœbe (*signing*) Through the floor.

Everyone joins in with the signs. As they do so:

  Fiona enters R carrying a photograph

Fiona (*to George*) That's the last photo I took of him. You can have
  it.

George looks and looks at the photo during the following

Duncan Through the floor.
Marion (*signing and saying*) I like. (*She says to Phœbe*) You.

*Phœbe shows the others how to sign "you". They all start saying
and signing "I like you" to each other*

Molly (*signing and saying*) I like autumn.
Marion (*signing and saying*) I like underclothes.
Fiona (*signing and saying*) I like spaghetti.

Phœbe shows each of them how to sign the new words they've used

George I like —— (*He can't speak for emotion and hugs the photo to him*)

Duncan (*signing and saying*) Singing.

George (*recovering*) And singing.

Duncan We both like singing.

Molly Go on then. Give us a song.

Duncan Yeh? (*He goes to George and looks at the photo; then he starts to sing Gilbert and Sullivan's A Policeman's Lot*) When a felon's not engaged in his employment ——

George (*joining in*) His employment.

They complete the song with actions for Phœbe's sake, to everyone's appreciation

Duncan (*to Phœbe; signing*) You couldn't hear it.

Phœbe (*signing*) I could hear it through your face, your lips and the floor. You've got such easy lips to understand. (*She writes*)

Molly (*looking over Phœbe's shoulder and reading*) "You've got such easy lips to understand."

Duncan is pleased. Phœbe writes

And that's her e-mail address.

Phœbe gives Duncan her e-mail address, then smiles and shakes Duncan's hand. She then shakes hands with all the others and heads for the exit L, happy. Everyone smiles and waves

Phœbe exits

Julie enters

Julie Have you all weighed-in then?

Molly Yes. No. Not quite. Nearly … (*She thinks she's cottoned on to a plan*) I think it's worked. I'm pretty sure they'll stay. (*She nods at the men*) I'll go and put the weighing-in music on.

Molly fairly skips off into the room R

Fiona Ooh, not looking forward to this …
George Remember what I said, Fiona …
Fiona What?
George Sexy.
Fiona Yes. Thank you, George.

Fiona, happy, breasts to the fore, exits into the room R

Julie All right, Marion?
Marion I … I …
Julie Have you told everyone now?
Marion Yes.
Julie Good. You'll go from strength to strength. Why don't we go
    to the dogs' home at Corn Hill this weekend? There might be a
    special four-legged feller looking out for you?
Marion Yes! Please!

Marion, happy, exits into the room R

Julie (*to Duncan and George*) Ready? (*She smiles*) Come on then.
    The weigh-in.

Julie, confident that the men will follow her, exits into the room R

*George looks at his photo of Ian Barry and Duncan looks at his piece
of paper with Phœbe's e-mail address on it. They look at each other*

George Well, I don't know where we've met before.
Duncan The thing is, are we going to meet again?
George *The thing is* …

There is a portentous pause

Are we going to be weighed or are we going to the pub?

No-one will ever know because ——

THE CURTAIN FALLS

FURNITURE AND PROPERTY LIST

On stage: Two small tables with information leaflets on them
               Chairs

Personal: **Julie**: photograph
               Fiona, Marion, Molly, Duncan: handkerchiefs
               Phœbe: notepad and pen
               Fiona: photograph

LIGHTING PLOT

Practical fittings required: nil
A waiting room. The same throughout

To open: General interior lighting

No cues

EFFECTS PLOT

Cue 1   **Molly** exits into the room R   (Page 21)
           Line dance music

Cue 2   **Phœbe** and **Duncan** join the dancing   (Page 23)
           Music swells